Books by Stephen Krensky

MAIDEN VOYAGE

Maiden Voyage

The Story of the Statue of Liberty

by STEPHEN KRENSKY

Illustrated by Richard Rosenblum

ATHENEUM

New York

1985

Library of Congress Cataloging-in-Publication Data

Krensky, Stephen.   *Maiden voyage.*

*SUMMARY: Discusses our Statue of Liberty's conception,
creation, and history.*
*1. Statue of Liberty (New York, N.Y.)—Juvenile
literature.   2. New York (N.Y.)—Statues—Juvenile
literature.   [1. Statue of Liberty National Monument
(New York, N.Y.)   2. Monuments]   I. Rosenblum,
Richard, ill.   II. Title.*
F128.64.L6K74   1985   974.7'1   85-7513
ISBN 0-689-31111-7

Text copyright © 1985 by Stephen Krensky
Pictures copyright © 1985 by Atheneum Publishers, Inc.
*Published simultaneously in Canada by
Collier Macmillan Canada, Inc.*
Composition by Dix Type, Inc., Syracuse, New York
*Printed and bound by
the Maple-Vail Publishing Company, Inc., Binghamton, New York*
Designed by Mary Ahern
First Edition

For my grandparents

MAIDEN VOYAGE

On July 4, 1776, when the American colonists declared their independence from England, they did not look to the Statue of Liberty for inspiration. But it wasn't their fault. There was not yet a statue to look to. When Robert Fulton took the first steamboat up the Hudson River in 1807, it was big news for an important port like New York. The statue, though, missed out on the excitement. In 1844, Samuel Morse invented the telegraph, and people were soon sending messages across the country in an instant. No one sent a word about the Statue of Liberty. There just wasn't anything to say.

Although the Statue of Liberty looks as if it has always stood in the middle of New York harbor, it hasn't. In fact, *Liberty* missed the first one hundred years of United States history. Not that anyone noticed it was missing. Clipper ships sailed past the spot daily, and none of the passengers ever complained. It's safe to say that had Americans been left to think of building the statue themselves, it never would have been built. *Liberty* was simply not a home-grown idea. Like fine wines and fashions, it was imported from France.

The idea was political at first. Ever since the French Revolution in 1789, France had been full of political ideas. In the next fifty years, the French had tried all kinds of leaders, including three kings and an emperor. In 1848, they elected Napoleon III to lead them, but he soon turned himself into an emperor, too. Napoleon III was more interested in power than popularity, and he ruled France with a heavy hand.

Many French people were upset about this. They couldn't get too upset in public because, if they did, Napoleon III would have them thrown in jail. But in private they spoke out. By the 1860s, some of these speakers had become well known. One of them was Edouard Laboulaye, a university professor in Paris. Laboulaye had a lot of friends, and they often got together to talk. Mostly they talked about politics and history, and they had a lot to say.

The professor had written many books about the United States, and he always spoke highly of it. He was proud that France had helped the Americans win their independence. He was glad, too, that the United States had succeeded so well, democratic government and all. Sadly, France had forgotten what democracy was like. Laboulaye wanted to refresh his country's memory. He would have to be careful, though. He didn't want to make Napoleon III angry. People who did that sometimes disappeared and were never heard from again.

Among Laboulaye's many guests in 1865 was Frederic Auguste Bartholdi. The thirty-one-year-old sculptor had not come to talk about politics. He had been hired to sculpt a portrait bust of Laboulaye. Still, he couldn't help listening while he worked, and what he heard made sense. Laboulaye insisted that France and the United States had shared a special friendship since the American Revolution. Bartholdi agreed. Laboulaye said France needed to be pushed in a more democratic direction. Bartholdi thought so, too. Laboulaye said that building a monument to Franco-American friendship was the best way to accomplish this. Bartholdi was not about to argue with him.

After all, monuments were Bartholdi's business. He had been a professional sculptor for ten years. Born in Alsace, he lived in Paris, where he had gone to school (taking him there had been his mother's idea—his father had died when Auguste was two years old). Young Auguste had been a very ordinary student. In many ways, he was a very ordinary sculptor, too. Art critics were not wild about his work. But art critics didn't buy much sculpture. The people who did thought Bartholdi was a clever and charming man. They enjoyed his company, and they liked to hire him.

In the Paris of the 1850s and 1860s there was a lot of hiring to be done. The city, long a medieval hodgepodge of narrow winding streets, was fast becoming a modern metropolis. Old buildings were coming down at a furious rate. New ones were going up even faster. Wide boulevards were being cut across the town, and park lands were being mapped out. A lot of statues and other stonework was needed to fill in courtyards and decorate the greenery.

Bartholdi did big projects and small ones, but he liked the big ones best. His dream was to do a huge project, something colossal like one of the pyramids. (He had first seen them on a trip to Egypt in 1856.) The pyramids did more than fit into their surroundings, they shaped the landscape itself.

Nobody was building pyramids anymore, but spectacular projects were still in the making. In 1867, Bartholdi took his second trip to Egypt, and there he gazed on a modern marvel —the almost completed Suez Canal. Even the ancient pharaohs would have been impressed with this 107-mile (178 kilometers) ditch cut from the Mediterranean Sea to the Gulf of Suez.

Most people were satisfied just to look at the canal and leave. Not Bartholdi. He wanted to help out. This was no vague notion on his part. He had an idea, a plan to build a lighthouse at the canal's mouth. Naturally this would not be any old lighthouse. It would have the form of an Egyptian peasant woman, her right arm holding a torch aloft.

Here was the challenge Bartholdi had searched for. He could easily envision its grace and beauty. He could also imagine its cost. The lighthouse would be very expensive. But Bartholdi didn't let that stop him. He went straight to Ismail Pasha, the ruler of Egypt. If anyone could afford the lighthouse, he could. Ismail Pasha listened to Bartholdi's proposal. Since it cost him nothing to encourage Bartholdi, he told the sculptor to develop the idea further. Bartholdi was thrilled. He went home a happy man.

Two years later, Bartholdi returned to Egypt with more complete plans. He was excited

about them. He thought Ismail Pasha would be excited, too. After all, the world would think great things of the man who commissioned such a spectacular lighthouse (and even greater things, Bartholdi hoped, of the man who had designed it).

The world never got the chance. Ismail Pasha dismissed Bartholdi's plan with barely a look. Very simply, the lighthouse no longer interested him. There was no argument, no further discussion, and Bartholdi had nowhere else to turn. Without Ismail Pasha's support, no lighthouse would be built.

Drooping and disappointed, Bartholdi returned to France. He had been so close. And it was possible that that might be the only really big project he would ever compete for. It was depressing to think about.

His attention, though, was soon drawn to other things. A war was brewing. For years the Prussians had been practicing for battle, and mostly they had practiced to battle with France. The French, on the other hand, didn't practice at all. But they still found the Prussians annoying. In the summer of 1870, France decided it was time to teach Prussia a lesson.

Bartholdi enlisted in the army. He was

made an officer and quickly sent home to help defend Alsace. He felt important in his uniform, and he liked visiting his mother, but he had little else to cheer about. The war was not going the way the French had planned. The Prussians were organized and disciplined. The French were not. In Alsace, on the Prussian border, the French situation looked bad. It soon looked even worse. When fifteen thousand Prussians advanced on the town, Major Bartholdi had only fifteen soldiers to command. What could he do? He was brave, but he was not stupid.

He told his men to retreat.

The Prussian victory was complete in six months. France limped to the peace table and made the best terms it could. As part of the settlement, France lost Alsace to the Prussians. Bartholdi was shocked. Almost overnight everything changed—the government, the language, the money, even the city streets. Each *rue* was now a *strasse* with a German name to match. When Bartholdi went home to visit, he felt like a foreigner in his own house.

Things were no better in Paris. The building boom had stopped. Almost everything had stopped. The war had created shortages of food and clothing. Crowds of angry citizens, hungry and humiliated, roamed the streets. Nobody was putting up new statues. The mobs were still busy tearing the old ones down.

Clearly France was an unhappy place to be, and Bartholdi was unhappy to be there. He wanted to get away. Bartholdi was a practical man, though. He didn't want a vacation; he wanted to take a trip that might further his career. Fortunately, he remembered Laboulaye's talk about creating a monument to Franco-American friendship. This was an idea that shouldn't go to waste.

Bartholdi went to see Laboulaye. It was time, he told the professor, that someone went to America to raise support for the monument. He was ready and willing. His bags could be packed in an instant. Laboulaye was sure they could, but that didn't mean he approved of the plan. He asked his friends for their opinions. They were skeptical of Bartholdi's offer. Was he really serious about the monument? Or was that just his excuse for going, a way of hunting up business in America? The more they thought about it, though, the more they realized there was no harm in Bartholdi looking for work abroad. If he wanted to make such a trip, they would not discourage him. More important, they agreed to write him letters of introduction to their influential American friends.

Bartholdi traveled to America in June, 1871. He spent the weeks on board ship studying books and maps about the United States. When the ship finally docked in New York, he was eager to stretch his legs. He had a full schedule, not only in New York, but in Boston and Washington as well. There were appointments by day and parties by night. Bartholdi met many famous magazine editors, writers, scientists, generals, and politicians. He talked, he listened, and he mentioned the monument to everyone.

Bartholdi saw a lot in his first weeks in America, but he wanted to see more. He soon headed west, visiting St. Louis, San Francisco and other cities. He had plenty of company along the way. Pioneers were crossing the frontier by rail, river, horseback, and covered wagon. Bartholdi drew pictures of them in his sketchbooks. What a place this America was! There was so much energy, so much hustle and bustle. It was hard to take it all in at once.

Everything he saw was big—the land, the people, the ideas. Even the buffaloes were big. How appropriate, he thought, for America to have a big statue, too. True, Americans did not

seem to get too excited about monuments (they had been fiddling with the Washington Monument for almost thirty years), but he was prepared to overlook that.

With high hopes, Bartholdi had even chosen a site for his statue—Bedloe's Island in New York harbor. Once owned by Isaack Bedloo, who had come to America from France in the 1600s, it was now federal property. A fort stood there, Fort Wood, but the army really wasn't using it anymore. The sea gulls were, but Bartholdi didn't stop to ask their opinion of the project. He was in too great a hurry to go home and get things started.

On his return, Bartholdi went to see Laboulaye at once. He said much in praise of the United States, for the trip had been a huge success. Clearly, the Americans were all in favor of a monument. He was ready to take the next step. What did the professor think it should be?

This was an awkward moment for Laboulaye. No one had expected Bartholdi to accomplish so much. It made it more difficult to rein in the young man's enthusiasm. But Laboulaye had no choice. This was no time to start planning a monument to Liberty. France was in a sorry state. Although Napoleon III and the old government had fallen at the war's end, the effects of war were less easy to erase. The economy was in ruins. Paris was staging its own little revolt, and people were starving in the streets. The new leaders could barely hold the country together, even using harsh and undemocratic controls. Nobody liked them, but nobody had any better suggestions to make, either.

Laboulaye and his friends, who opposed these steps in principle, had supported them for the good of France. So they thought they would look pretty silly trying to create a monument to Liberty right now. Such a crusade would be doomed to failure. It would get no support from politicians or anyone else.

Bartholdi could only shake his head in discouragement. First Egypt and now this. Whenever he got excited about a project, it slipped through his fingers. Still, all was not lost. Laboulaye had said he was glad the trip had gone well. And he hadn't told Bartholdi to give up. He had only told him to be patient. They would both have to wait for the right time to come.

Bartholdi waited and waited and waited. He managed to keep busy with other work, but it wasn't easy. *Liberty* was often in his thoughts. One year turned into two, then three, then four. Bartholdi began to wonder if the right moment would ever arrive.

Finally, it did. By 1875, conditions in France had greatly improved. In that year the Franco-American Union was formed. It was led by Laboulaye and other Frenchmen with ties to the United States. Their goal, announced at a dinner on November 6, 1875, was to get the Statue of Liberty built. Of course, this announcement was just the beginning. The appeal for money came next. This appeal was not aimed at a few wealthy donors (although their money was welcome), it was aimed at the general population. Laboulaye and his friends were still hoping that *Liberty* would inspire democratic thoughts in the French people. For that to happen, the funds would have to come from them.

Over two hundred thousand francs (forty thousand dollars) were quickly collected in towns all over the country. Much more was needed, but Bartholdi remained hopeful. Sculptors were always fighting for funds. The important thing was to keep the project alive, and trust that luck would be on his side.

As it happened, a little luck was at hand. The United States was about to throw itself a one hundredth birthday party in Philadelphia. A lot of countries were being invited, and France was among them. The guests were bringing exhibits instead of gifts, something Bartholdi was quick to take note of. If the statue, or at least part of the statue (there was neither time nor money to finish the whole thing), could be part of the French display, it would help build support for *Liberty* in America. But getting the statue included would not necessarily be easy. Bartholdi asked Laboulaye and others to speak to the right people and say the right things. They did a good job. When the official French delegation and exhibits sailed for America, Bartholdi and *Liberty's* upraised arm and torch went with them.

The year 1876 ushered in the birth of organized baseball, *The Adventures of Tom Sawyer,* and the invention of the telephone. The year's most publicized event, though, was the Centennial Exhibition in Philadelphia. In an era famous for business and industry, the giant celebration mostly sidestepped art and culture. It featured signs of progress like the typewriter and the refrigerated railroad car. Nearly fifty countries had displays spread out over one hundred sixty-seven buildings. The main building itself covered twenty acres.

With so much to look at, Bartholdi's arm and torch still managed to stick out. Many of the nine million people who passed through the Exhibition stopped to stare at it. The more curious spectators climbed up the stairs inside the arm and emerged on a platform around the flame. They had a good view from there, but not everyone was impressed. Some people thought the arm and torch was dumb. It looked incomplete, they said. (They didn't realize it was only part of the proposed monument.) Other critics sniffed disapprovingly over *Liberty's* purpose—to celebrate Franco-American friendship. They didn't care that France had helped out during the Revolution. That was ancient history. What had France done for America lately?

It wasn't Bartholdi's job to answer this question. He focused his attention on the visitors who liked his work. There were plenty of them. These people were flattered that the French were going to so much trouble at their own expense.

Bartholdi had explained, of course, that France was only supplying the statue itself. The

pedestal base was to be designed by Americans and built with American money. People nodded when he said that, but nobody stepped forward to take charge. This didn't worry Bartholdi. All the Americans needed was a little push in the right direction. So, after the Exhibition ended, he took the arm and torch to New York. Properly displayed, he thought, it would surely help the fund-raising get started.

He was wrong about that. The arm and torch was poorly received in its corner of Madison Square Park. New Yorkers were used to seeing statues of generals on horseback or well-dressed statesmen standing at attention. They had never seen a statue like this. Nobody built a statue in parts. People wondered if Bartholdi was serious. The city newspapers hinted at fraud. Was this whole statue business a hoax? Was Bartholdi going to run off with the pedestal fund at his first chance?

Bartholdi was planning no such thing. Where did people get these ideas? He often had the same problem in France. Whenever a statue was proposed, there were always people who complained and criticized and carried on. In the end, though, they came around. Why? Because of their pride. They couldn't take the chance that a statue they turned down might turn up somewhere else.

Bartholdi figured that New Yorkers were as proud as anyone else. He had no wish to put *Liberty* anywhere but Bedloe's Island, but he was willing to *pretend* he was considering a change. Therefore he made an announcement. If New York didn't want the statue, he said, another site would be found. He wasn't going to beg. There were plenty of other places to choose from. Philadelphia, for example, had long shown interest . . .

Suddenly the grumblers disappeared. As Bartholdi expected, New York was not about to be upstaged by Philadelphia or anywhere else. No offense had been meant, the newspapers assured Bartholdi. The arm and torch was perfectly respectable. Nothing could be more proper.

Bartholdi graciously accepted all the praise and apologies. New York was indeed the best site for *Liberty,* he admitted. Naturally, that only helped up to a point. The city would still need a pedestal for the statue to stand on.

New York now understood that. William Evarts, the American Secretary of State, formed a committee in July, 1877. It was made up of rich or prominent New Yorkers. Many of them were both. They were supposed to raise money for the pedestal. Instead they busied themselves writing to their powerful friends in Washington. A project like this, they thought, should involve the federal government.

Their powerful friends agreed, but only up to a point. Congress soon pledged funds to maintain the monument if and when the statue was

built. That *if* and *when* were largely overlooked by Evarts's committee. The members were pleased. They smoked their expensive cigars and patted each other on the back. How easy it had been to take care of the statue's future. Amid all the cigar smoke, though, their original problem remained—raising money for the pedestal. Congress, after all, had pledged nothing to seeing that the statue was built. Somehow, nobody seemed to be worried about that.

Bartholdi couldn't worry about it, either. He had money problems of his own. *Liberty's* supporters had squeezed out every patriotic franc they could find in the French countryside. They had even sold two hundred small copies of the statue in France and the United States. More money was needed. A lot more. Donations alone would not bring in enough. The Franco-American Union needed to create some new excitement in the campaign. But how? What would stir the French people into giving as they had never given before?

The answer was a lottery. This was no small event or even a local one. It was a big deal. The Franco-American Union promoted it all over the country. Tickets were priced at one franc (twenty cents) each. Winners won prizes, but they didn't have to worry about going home with something they hated. If they didn't like their prize, they could have its cash value instead.

The lottery was very popular. Some people bought tickets to win prizes; others bought tickets to win money. Whatever the reason, a lot of tickets were sold—three hundred thousand in all. News of the lottery helped bring in other contributions as well. By July, 1881, two million francs (four hundred thousand dollars) had been collected, enough to see the statue completed.

Through the years Bartholdi had been raising funds, he also had worked on *Liberty's* design. Ancient artists had portrayed Liberty as a woman in flowing robes. What was good enough for the Greeks and Romans was good enough for Bartholdi. His sketches and drawings followed in their tradition.

His statue, though, was going to do more than just stand around. Like his idea for the Suez Canal, Bartholdi planned *Liberty* as a lighthouse. In her raised right hand she would hold a torch. In her left hand, she would hold a symbol of freedom. But which symbol should it be? He tried a broken vase in one clay model and broken chains in another. Though the Greeks and Romans had used them both, neither struck Bartholdi as quite right. He wanted *Liberty* to be classical, but he wanted it clearly linked to American liberty, too. In the end, he put a simple tablet in the left hand. Its inscription read JULY IV MDCCLXXVI—the date of the Declaration of Independence.

Meanwhile, there was also *Liberty's* face to decide on. Should it be plain or beautiful? Should she look stern or friendly? Other artists had pictured Liberty as a beautiful goddess or a strong peasant woman. Bartholdi saw his *Liberty* as a little of both. The problem was finding the right model for his image.

He solved this problem with his mother's help. She had always been a strong and proud figure—what better model for *Liberty* could there be? He needed her permission, of course, and he got it. No doubt she enjoyed telling her friends. It wasn't every son who immortalized his mother in a statue the size of an office building. Yet while Madame Bartholdi was pleased to be a model, she was still unhappily living in Alsace under Prussian rule. So *Liberty's* gaze was not a smiling one.

Once Bartholdi finished his design, he was ready to sculpt the statue itself. He couldn't just start carving his 151 foot (46 meters) statue from a mountain stone, though. No such mountains were handy, and besides, a statue like that could never be moved. Its great size also made it too heavy and expensive to be cast in bronze. Bartholdi had to take another approach. The one he picked had been first used two hundred years earlier in Italy. The process was called repoussé, and it involved placing hammered copper sheets over a skeleton of wood, iron, or stone.

His first step was to build a small plaster model of the statue. It was one-sixteenth *Liberty's* projected size, a little over nine feet (three meters) high. This was no rough copy of *Liberty*. It was a precise model, complete in every detail. Next, he divided it into three hundred sections. Three measurements (length, height, and depth) were taken from many points on each section. These measurements were checked very carefully (There were more than nine thousand of them in all.) Each one was then multiplied by four.

With these enlarged figures, Bartholdi accurately built another model four times bigger —one-fourth the actual size. Again the model was divided into sections, again the measurements were taken, and again these measurements were multiplied by four. These final figures were the ones Bartholdi used to construct the statue itself.

His workshop was a busy place, crowded with carpenters, metalworkers, and modelers. The air was filled with a hundred conversations and a lot of plaster dust. Bartholdi kept careful track of *Liberty's* progress. He roamed through the huge room answering questions and checking everyone's work.

As the models grew bigger, some changes were made. What looked good at one size did not always look good at another. The crook of an arm, the shape of a nostril, the length of a finger —anything might need a slight adjustment. Bartholdi had many assistants to help him, but he made all the artistic decisions himself. For months and months he was a very busy man.

There was no way of putting together the statue's full-sized plaster cast—it was simply too big. So it sat in large pieces—the head here, an arm there—around Bartholdi's workshop. From these pieces, *Liberty's* skin was shaped. Long copper sheets were cut into plates that skilled workers could handle. Then the workers hammered and bent the copper plates against the plaster

casts using wooden mallets and levers. It was delicate work. The plates were only 3/32 inch (2.4 mm) thick. As each one was finished, it was numbered to mark its location. That way there would be no later confusion about which piece went where.

Creating *Liberty* was more than a matter of art alone, though. Bartholdi needed a metal framework to hold up the copper plates. He also needed an engineer to design it. His first engineer died before the planning had gone very far. The second was forty-seven-year-old Alexandre Gustave Eiffel. Eiffel was already famous in France for doing the impossible—building railroad bridges in places where people thought it couldn't be done. In another ten years, he would become famous all over the world for designing something besides a bridge—the Eiffel Tower.

For the moment, though, the Statue of Liberty had his full attention. *Liberty's* size and shape presented a big problem for an engineer. Anything that large, with a raised arm projecting outward, would need a lot of support. Since the statue would have no exterior lines or buttresses, all the support would have to come from the inside. What interior structure would be strong enough to do the job?

This was a question Eiffel had answered before. The stresses on *Liberty* were much like the ones on his railroad bridges. What worked for a bridge, thought Eiffel, could be made to work for a statue, too. Along these lines, he designed an iron skeleton that looked something like a railroad bridge seen inside out. The web of iron pylons might be ugly, but it was secure.

Eiffel knew his framework would last for many decades. He was less sure about the copper plates that would cover it. Wind, rain, snow, heat, cold and saltwater would all buffet them in turn. To withstand these forces the plates had to be held securely. On the other hand, the plates needed flexibility, too. If they were held too tightly, they would quickly crack from severe heat or cold and fall down. It was a tricky situation. The plates had to be held just right.

After some experimenting, Eiffel devised a solution. He did not connect the copper plates directly to the iron framework. Instead he joined them to a series of straps and bars. It was the straps and bars that he attached to the framework itself. They held the plates firmly but still allowed them to expand or contract, to bend or ripple slightly. Anchored in this way, he thought, the plates would survive a long time in New York's open air.

It was the open air of France, though, that

surrounded *Liberty's* first outing. She was fully assembled on the outskirts of Paris a year before she came to America. The construction took place in the foundry yards of Gaget, Gauthier & Company. It did not take place in secret. The statue was much too big for that. In fact, on pleasant Sundays in 1883, many Parisians packed picnic lunches and went out to check *Liberty's* progress. As the months passed, the statue grew and grew. By early 1884, it towered above the surrounding buildings. It was now so tall that some people could watch the construction without leaving home.

On July 4, 1884, amid speeches and refreshments, the finished statue was officially presented to the United States. The American ambassador to France declared his thanks for the gift. He was proud to accept it on behalf of his country, but he didn't actually take *Liberty* home with him. The 225 tons of statue were a little hard to move.

For five months, *Liberty* stood on display in the foundry yard. Then, in December, 1884, the workers who had put her together began to take her apart. The copper plates were removed; the iron framework was dismantled. It took months to dissect, label, and load everything into huge

wooden cases. Once the 210 cases were ready, a 70-car train carried them to the port of Rouen. There the warship *Isère* was waiting to take the crates to America.

Liberty was on her way at last. But was New York ready for her arrival? It had been ready for telephones in 1877 and electric lights in 1882. New York had elevated trains and the theaters of Broadway. It had millions of people, and it was peopled by millionaires. New York thought of itself as being ready for anything.

It was not ready for *Liberty*. It was not even almost ready. True, the American committee had hired the well-known architect Richard Morris Hunt to design the statue's pedestal. And the construction had been started. A huge hole had been dug in the middle of Fort Wood, 53 feet (16 meters) deep and 91 feet (28 meters) square at the bottom. It was a little smaller, 65 feet (20 meters) square, at the top. The deep hole was then filled with concrete. Lots of concrete. There was only a 10-foot (3-meter) square open shaft in the middle.

The foundation was very sturdy; nobody had any doubts about that. It was just the sort of foundation *Liberty's* pedestal should have. The trouble was, there was no money left to build much of the pedestal itself. Evarts's committee had already spent the $125,000 they had, and only 15 feet of the 89-foot-high pedestal was done.

The committee had tried raising funds from auctions, theatrical benefits, even prize fights. The response had been lukewarm at best. These events needed ordinary people to support them, and ordinary people weren't interested in doing that. After all, nobody was inviting them to fancy dinners to discuss the fancy plans for the statue. If only the bigwigs were going to be there, then they could pay for that privilege themselves.

At one point Bartholdi had returned to New York to try to help out. Had the committee tried raising money in other parts of the country, he asked? After all, the French funds had come from 181 different towns. The committee members took his suggestion, and they attempted to mount a national campaign. It failed. Americans at large had no real affection for the statue. They saw *Liberty* as a gift from France to New York. Surely, they thought, such a big and prosperous city could afford to pay for its own pedestal.

Maybe so, but big and prosperous New York was dragging its feet. As late as 1883, the pedestal was a long way from being built. In fact, the project showed signs of going completely down the drain. What *Liberty* needed was a high-minded benefactor to write out a very large check. What *Liberty* got was the New York *World*. This newspaper had been recently bought by Joseph Pulitzer, a Hungarian immigrant who already owned the St. Louis *Post-Dispatch*. Pulitzer had made the *Post-Dispatch* a success by building up its circulation. He was itching to do the same with the *World*. To draw the interest of new readers, he needed an issue that would attract their attention. *Liberty's* pedestal campaign made an inviting target.

Pulitzer took aim and fired. He denounced the feeble efforts of Evarts's committee. All its members wanted to do was eat, drink, and hope for the best. Well, that was no way to build a statue pedestal. The *World* would show them how to do it. The newspaper began a drive to collect funds from its readers. Pulitzer was full of confidence. He thought his campaign would succeed without much effort. To spur on contributions, though, the *World* promised to print the name of any donor giving a dollar or more.

The campaign sounded good on paper, but it just didn't work. Only a few thousand dollars

JOSEPH PULITZER

came in. Apparently people weren't very eager to see their names in print. Pulitzer let the matter drop. He had other things to do, like getting Grover Cleveland elected president.

By early 1885, $25,000 more had been raised; another $125,000 was needed. The whole business was becoming embarrassing. Dozens of New York millionaires could have paid for the pedestal without losing any sleep. Some of them were even on Evarts's committee. None of them stepped forward. The city, state, and federal governments also refused to save the day. Other cities were not so shy. Philadelphia, Boston, Baltimore, even distant Minneapolis loudly offered to take the statue off New York's hands.

Meanwhile the crates were being packed in Paris.

Enough was enough. Pulitzer had been distracted by the Presidential election, but with Grover Cleveland safely in the White House, he decided to try again. In March, 1885, the *World* started a new campaign. Pulitzer had learned from his earlier effort that the problem was *Liberty's* image. The statue was too closely tied to the High and Mighty. Pulitzer had to change that perception. He had failed before with a simple appeal. This time he would grab the public's attention and hold on till the job was done.

Stories and editorials began pouring from the *World's* presses. *Liberty* was no plaything of the rich, the paper declared. It was a gift to all Americans, to the American spirit, to the American way of life. The *World* pulled no patriotic punches. Everyone had a stake in the statue, and *any* amount would be welcome to aid the pedestal fund.

The campaign paid off. Small donations began to arrive by the thousands. Nickels and dimes flooded the *World's* offices, many of them from boys and girls. These children often sent in letters with their spare change. The *World* was quick to print them, hoping to draw even more contributions. The letters were always short and cute, and the ones from poor children were especially touching. Many of these notes, in fact, seemed too good to be true. Some of them probably were. Who knows how many were invented by the *World* staff? But fake or real, they were a success. On August 11, 1885, the paper announced that $102,000 had been raised. There were 121,000 donors in all.

Now the pedestal construction could continue. The walls went up, made of concrete to save money, but covered with a thin granite shell for the sake of appearances. They ranged from 8 to 19 feet (2.5 to 6 meters) thick. The base was

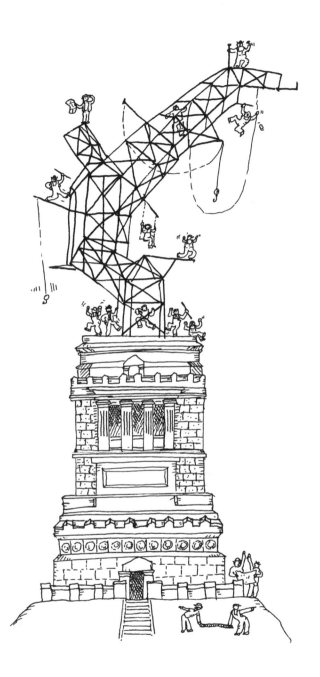

65 feet (20 meters) square at the bottom and 43 feet (13 meters) square at the top. All together, 27,000 tons (24,489 metric tons) of concrete made up the foundation and pedestal. To help keep that concrete where it belonged, the walls were reinforced with steel beams laid side to side at the top and bottom.

The *Isère* had long since unloaded its cargo, which had been sitting in storage for months. Now Eiffel's iron skeleton was unpacked, and work began on reassembling it. The skeleton was very precise. Each piece of the framework was made to fit in one place and one place only. And every piece was clearly labeled. It was soon discovered, though, that some pieces did not fit where their labels said they would.

Naturally, the workers were upset by this. Some of them yelled, some of them kicked the ground, and probably a few got terrible headaches. But they still had to finish the statue. So once everyone calmed down, they continued the project. Large cranes moved the mislabeled pieces around like parts of a giant jigsaw puzzle. Finally, everything was properly put together. Bartholdi's copper plates were then joined to the skeleton (with the help of 300,000 copper rivets), and the statue was complete.

Well, almost complete. All the money the *World* had raised was gone. Everyone had assumed that when this happened, the statue would be finished. It wasn't. The torch still had to be lit. That would take more than matches; it would take lamps, wires, and generators. What was Evarts' committee to do? It was too embarrassed to ask the *World* for more money. Of course, none of its members wanted to pay for the torch, either. Luckily, the American Electric Manufacturing Company decided to contribute the necessary parts and services. *Liberty* could now shine forth on schedule.

October 28, 1886, was a holiday in New York City. Twenty thousand people marched down Broadway in a big parade. Across the East River, the City of Brooklyn closed its schools. The holiday, the parade, and the closed schools were all in honor of the statue. When the parade ended, the people who had marched in it, and many who hadn't, went down to the harbor. The harbor itself was full of ships, and the ships full of passengers. They had not come for the misty weather. They had not come because they liked long speeches. They had come to see *Liberty's* face unveiled.

Twenty-five hundred guests arrived for the

ceremonies on Bedloe's Island. President Cleveland, the Secretaries of State, War, Navy, and Interior, and many French dignitaries were all there. Bartholdi was not with them. He was standing high overhead inside *Liberty's* torch. He was also holding a rope. The rope was supporting a huge French flag in front of *Liberty's* face.

Naturally Bartholdi was very excited. He had been waiting fifteen years for this day. He had a good view of the speakers below, and the many people and boats lining the harbor. His hands gripped the rope tightly. When the last speech was finished, he would release the rope, and the flag would drop away. It was too bad he couldn't hear the speakers, but he had been prepared for that. When the time came to let go of the rope, he would be signaled from below.

The first speaker was Vicomte Ferdinand de Lesseps, head of the Franco-American Union, and the man also responsible for the building of the Suez Canal. He said the dignified things everyone expected. The second was William Evarts, the head of the American pedestal committee, and now a United States Senator. Evarts had prepared a long speech intending to make the most of his captive audience. He was an experienced speaker, but he was used to speaking

indoors. On windy Bedloe's Island, he had to shout for his words to carry. After a few loud sentences, he paused to rest his voice.

The boy appointed to signal Bartholdi was very nervous. This was a big day for him, too. He was much too nervous to keep careful track of the speakers. When Senator Evarts paused, the boy thought he was done. The boy thought everyone was done. This was the time for the signal. He waved his white handkerchief overhead.

Inside the torch, Bartholdi saw the handkerchief. He promptly let go of the rope. As Evarts started up again, the flag fell, and *Liberty's* face was revealed. Whistles and cheers drowned out his words. He finished the speech anyway.

President Cleveland was the last to speak. Unlike the senator, he knew that no one was paying attention to him. Therefore he had the good sense to keep his remarks very brief.

The unveiling was marked with a twenty-one-gun salute. *Liberty Enlightening the World* (the statue's official name) was well worth it. She stood 151 feet (46 meters) high. The torch flame rose 305 feet (93 meters) above sea level. The arm holding the torch was itself 42 feet (13 meters) long. The face was 10 feet (3 meters) wide with eyes 2.5 feet (.8 meters) across.

Bartholdi was pleased to see *Liberty* settled at last in her proper place. His only regret was that his mother and Professor Laboulaye were missing the dedication. (His mother had been too old to make the trip and Laboulaye had died in 1883.) Still, Bartholdi enjoyed the continuing celebration. He was honored at a big dinner that night, and wealthy New Yorkers turned out in force for the event. Most of them had done nothing to help the statue get off the ground, but they never missed a good party if they could help it.

The New Yorkers who didn't attend the party had mixed reactions to the statue. Some liked it. Some didn't. Many people didn't care about it one way or the other. A few of them still thought the gift was silly. They didn't believe that there were such friendly ties between the United States and France, and certainly none worth making such a fuss about.

Silly or not, *Liberty* was meant to be a symbol of Franco-American friendship and a prod to French democracy. That at least was the aim of its French supporters. But their aim soon went astray. By the time Bartholdi died in 1904, the original symbolism was lost. Although the statue had many American visitors, *Liberty* was making her greatest impression on the poor people moving to the United States from abroad. These immigrants were from many countries with different languages and different customs, but they left behind similar lives of sorrow or desperation. They didn't care about France, French politics, or Franco-American friendship. They cared only about starting a new life in America. As they sailed into New York, huddled on the lower decks of large ships, the Statue of Liberty loomed up before them. She stood there to welcome them, they thought, and it was a greeting they would always remember.

In 1883, Emma Lazarus, a thirty-seven-

year-old New York poet, had written a poem about the statue called "The New Colossus." She wrote it upon hearing of a wave of violent attacks against Jews in Eastern Europe. These pogroms were driving their victims to America in record

numbers. For Lazarus, *Liberty* was the "Mother of Exiles" welcoming these weary travelers from abroad. She was a figure who boldly declared:

> *. . . Give me your tired, your poor,*
> *Your huddled masses yearning to breathe free,*
> *The wretched refuse of your teeming shore,*
> *Send these, the homeless, tempest-tost, to me,*
> *I lift up my lamp beside the golden door.*

The poem received little attention at first. But the immigrants kept coming. Millions of them entered the country at Ellis Island within sight of the statue. In the following decades, the United States truly became the "Mother of Exiles," and *Liberty* was the image of that mother. The poem and the statue became so entwined that in 1903 a plaque bearing the words of "The New Colossus" was put up in *Liberty's* base.

Americans were now clearly proud of the statue. Nobody grumbled anymore about it being a gift from France because most people had forgotten that it was. In their minds, the statue was, and always had been, an American symbol.

The federal government did not entirely share their pride. For many years, responsibility for the statue was passed around like excess baggage. *Liberty* was first run by the Lighthouse

Board because the lighted torch was supposed to be an aid to navigation. As a lighthouse, however, the statue never amounted to much. The torch light wasn't very strong, and ships had better landmarks to steer by.

In 1901, the Lighthouse Board gave the statue to the War Department because *Liberty* was standing on top of Fort Wood (which still belonged to the army). In 1933, the War Department gave the statue to the National Park Service because the army didn't think it would ever use the fort again. Fortunately, the National Park Service was glad to have it and has kept it ever since.

Although immigrants no longer land at Ellis Island, the Statue of Liberty remains an important part of our national folklore. Over one million sightseers visit it every year. Many of them also visit the Museum of Immigration that was established in the statue's base.

Exposure to air and water turned *Liberty's* copper skin green long ago, but more than the statue's color changed through the years. Although it received a couple of baths, night lighting, and a few spot repairs, *Liberty* was largely left untended for almost a century. Over time, the plates and skeleton suffered serious damage from the steady pounding of nature. In the 1970s, a careful examination revealed what a sadly neglected statue *Liberty* had become. There were holes in the copper plates and rust in the ironwork that held them. The center of Eiffel's framework needed only a thorough cleaning, but the straps and bars, as well as the torch, needed to be completely replaced. Had these repairs been ignored, *Liberty* would have soon become not a monument but a monumental ruin. Fortunately, steps were taken to prevent this. Public and private donations were collected to rehabilitate the statue in time for its hundredth birthday.

After a full century, Bartholdi would be pleased to see *Liberty* still drawing so much attention. The statue certainly has no cause to complain. *Liberty Enlightening the World* may no longer stand for the ideals Bartholdi intended, but it has already gained a large piece of the immortality he wished for it.

INDEX